YOU SHOULD MEET

Yayoi Kusama

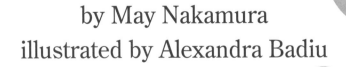

by May Nakamura

illustrated by Alexandra Badiu

Ready-to-Read

Simon Spotlight
New York London Toronto Sydney New Delhi

SIMON SPOTLIGHT

An imprint of Simon & Schuster Children's Publishing Division

1230 Avenue of the Americas, New York, New York 10020

This Simon Spotlight edition August 2021

Text copyright © 2021 by Simon & Schuster, Inc.

Illustrations copyright © 2021 by Alexandra Badiu

All rights reserved, including the right of reproduction in whole or in part in any form.

SIMON SPOTLIGHT, READY-TO-READ, and colophon are registered trademarks of Simon & Schuster, Inc.

For information about special discounts for bulk purchases, please contact Simon & Schuster Special Sales at
1-866-506-1949 or business@simonandschuster.com.

Manufactured in the United States of America 0721 LAK

2 4 6 8 10 9 7 5 3 1

Library of Congress Cataloging-in-Publication Data

Names: Nakamura, May, author.

Title: Yayoi Kusama / by May Nakamura.

Description: New York : Simon Spotlight, 2021. | Series: You should meet | Includes bibliographical references. |
Contents: Early Sketches—Journey to the United States—The Princess of Polka Dots—Return to Japan—You
Can't Stop Yayoi—But Wait . . . There's More! | Summary: "Get to know Yayoi Kusama, a Japanese artist known
for her extensive use of polka dots and for her infinity installations, in this fascinating nonfiction Level 3
Ready-to-Read, part of a series of biographies about people "you should meet!""—Provided by publisher.

Identifiers: LCCN 2021015058 (print) | LCCN 2021015059 (ebook) | ISBN 9781534495654 (hardcover) |
ISBN 9781534495647 (paperback) | ISBN 9781534495661 (ebook)

Subjects: LCSH: Kusama, Yayoi—Juvenile literature. | Artists—Japan—Biography—Juvenile literature. |
Women artists—Japan—Biography—Juvenile literature.

Classification: LCC N7359.K87 N35 2021 (print) | LCC N7359.K87 (ebook) | DDC 709.2 [B]—dc23

LC record available at https://lccn.loc.gov/2021015058

LC ebook record available at https://lccn.loc.gov/2021015059

CONTENTS

Introduction

Have you ever felt inspired by a beautiful piece of art? Maybe it was a drawing, a sculpture, or a book.

If so, you should meet Yayoi Kusama (say: yah-YO-ee koo-SAH-mah). Yayoi is an artist who has been making art for over eighty years. She paints, writes, makes sculptures, and fills rooms with mirrors and polka dots. Yayoi is one of the most famous female artists in the world.

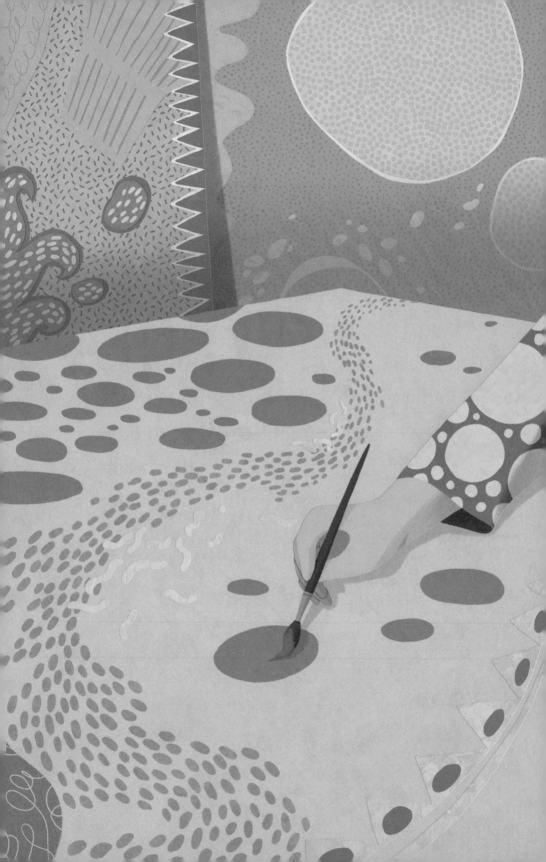

Yayoi didn't become famous overnight. Throughout her life, Yayoi had to work hard and overcome many obstacles. However, she never stopped following her dreams. Now her artwork is admired all over the world.

Once you meet Yayoi, you will be inspired to always do what you love too!

Chapter 1
Early Sketches

Yayoi Kusama was born on March 22, 1929, in Matsumoto (say: mah-tsu-MOE-toe), a town in Japan surrounded by tall mountains and blue sky. She had two older brothers and one older sister. Her family grew many flowers and vegetables on their land. As a little girl, Yayoi would spend hours drawing pumpkins, peonies, and anything else that was growing outside.

When Yayoi was ten years old, World War II began. Yayoi's parents were wealthy, so the war did not hurt them as much as it hurt other families in Japan. Still, the Japanese government required Yayoi to start working in a factory that made parachutes for the Japanese soldiers. Sometimes she worked for twelve hours a day, which left little time for her to draw.

One day, Yayoi was sitting outside with her sketchbook. Suddenly she became convinced that the violet flowers were talking to her! Yayoi ran back inside the house as fast as she could. Over the years, she would continue to have similar hallucinations—which means that she heard and saw things that didn't exist in real life.

Yayoi didn't want to talk to her friends or family about her hallucinations. What if they didn't believe her? Instead she made many paintings and drawings. Yayoi painted so much that she often ran out of canvases to use. Then she would paint on old cloth bags.

Yayoi's mother was not happy about Yayoi's art. Like many other people at the time, Yayoi's mother did not think that women were meant to be artists. She wanted her daughter to marry a rich man and become a mother.

Yayoi had other plans. Her parents argued a lot, and after seeing her parents' unhappy marriage, she did not want to get married. Her dream was to become an artist, no matter what her mother said!

Chapter 2
Journey to the United States

After World War II ended, Yayoi studied Japanese painting at a school in Kyoto, Japan. At first she was excited to leave home and attend art school. But before long, she became bored with the old-fashioned art styles that her teachers encouraged.

Meanwhile, Yayoi's mother continued to disapprove of her art. Yayoi realized that if she wanted to become a true artist, she would need to leave Japan.

Around that time, Yayoi was looking inside a small bookstore when she found a beautiful book of paintings. The painter's name was Georgia O'Keeffe. At the time, Georgia was one of the most famous American painters.

Yayoi decided to write a letter to Georgia. She asked for advice on becoming a successful painter. She also included several of her best watercolor paintings.

Yayoi was amazed when Georgia wrote back to her. What's more, Georgia liked her paintings! This encouraged Yayoi even more to pursue her art and to move to the United States.

Yayoi left Japan on November 11, 1957, when she was twenty-eight years old. She first arrived in Seattle, Washington. Then she moved to New York City.

After arriving, Yayoi visited the top of the Empire State Building. There she gazed at New York's glittering lights and tall buildings. Looking out at the city, she felt like she could accomplish anything.

But New York City was very different from Matsumoto. The streets were loud and busy, and did not feel welcoming for a young Japanese woman.

Yayoi wrote another letter to Georgia. Again, to her amazement, Georgia wrote back. The famous painter invited Yayoi to live with her in New Mexico, where it was much quieter. The invitation was very tempting, but New York City was the center of the art world. Yayoi knew she would need to stay there if she wanted to truly achieve her dreams.

A few years passed, and Yayoi continued to paint. One day, her telephone rang. It was Georgia, who was visiting New York City and wanted to meet Yayoi! Yayoi felt grateful to meet someone she admired so much. Meeting Georgia was a dream come true for Yayoi.

Chapter 3
The Princess of Polka Dots

In 1959, Yayoi displayed five paintings in her first New York exhibition. The canvases were completely covered in small, repeated strokes. They looked like nets stretched across the canvases. No one had ever seen paintings like these before.

Painting repetitive patterns was nothing new for Yayoi, though. She had been drawing and painting polka dots since she was a little girl. A polka dot is one of a series of round dots repeated on fabric to form a pattern. Many of Yayoi's hallucinations involved polka dots.

As Yayoi became popular in New York City, some people began to call her "the Princess of Polka Dots."

Yayoi thought that everything was a polka dot. The sun was a polka dot, the Earth was a polka dot, and so were the other planets. Even *she* was just one polka dot living among the millions of other people in the world. When she painted polka dots, Yayoi felt connected with all the other dots in the universe.

Yayoi kept on coming up with creative ideas. In 1963, she made posters out of a photograph of her sculpture. Then she covered the walls of her exhibition with these posters, making a patterned wallpaper. Andy Warhol, an American artist who was Yayoi's friend, but also her rival, came to see her work. Andy told Yayoi that her exhibit was fantastic.

Three years later, Andy covered his own exhibition walls with a repeated cow pattern. He had used Yayoi's idea and pretended it was his own. Other male artists also copied

Yayoi's art but didn't give her credit for being the first person to come up with the ideas. This made her angry and upset. It didn't stop her from making more art, though. She made sculptures, created films, and put on performances. The performances were called "Kusama Happenings" because they happened anywhere, at any time.

Yayoi also made clothes. Some of the dresses were designed to fit two people inside!

In 1966, everyone was talking about the
Venice Biennale, a famous art festival in
Italy. Yayoi didn't receive an invitation, but
she paid no attention. She flew to Venice
and set up 1,500 large mirror balls outside
the festival. She dressed up in a gold
kimono with a silver sash. Then she started

selling the mirror balls to people walking by, for two dollars each.

The festival guards quickly shut down her unplanned exhibit, but the event caused quite a commotion. Even though it wasn't officially part of the Biennale, Yayoi's exhibit became the talk of the town!

Chapter 4
Return to Japan

In 1973, Yayoi visited Tokyo, Japan. She had been feeling unwell, and she became even more ill during the trip. Instead of returning to New York, Yayoi remained in Tokyo and went to a hospital.

She and her doctors decided a good living arrangement would be for Yayoi to have her own room and live at the hospital, where she would get lots of help and care from medical staff. Every day from ten in the morning until six at night, she worked in her art studio.

Yayoi had had some success as an artist in America. Back at home, though, her artwork was mostly misunderstood. People found her shocking and disturbing. Some Japanese magazines even published gossip and lies about her.

Yayoi just kept creating art. In 1977, she began to publish stories and poems. They became very popular in Japan. One of her novels even won an award.

Then, twenty-seven years after showing up uninvited, Yayoi was officially invited to the 1993 Venice Biennale! What's more, she was the first Japanese artist to have an exhibition there all to herself.

For the Biennale, Yayoi made many pumpkin sculptures covered in polka dots. Then she covered the walls of the room with mirrors, making it seem like there were pumpkins everywhere! Yayoi called this type of exhibition an "Infinity Mirror room" because the mirror reflections made it seem like the room stretched out forever.

Yayoi continued to break new ground in the art world. In 2006, she became the first Japanese woman to receive the Praemium Imperiale. It is one of the highest honors given by the Japanese imperial family. Ten years later, she received the Order of Culture, another prestigious award, given to people who make important contributions to Japanese culture.

After so many years, the whole world finally loved Yayoi's artwork!

Chapter 5
You Can't Stop Yayoi

Today Yayoi's popularity has reached celebrity status. Tickets for her exhibitions sell out within an hour. Some fans sleep in tents outside her exhibitions, hoping for a chance to go inside. When Mexico City held an exhibition in 2015, the crowds were so large that the museum had to stay open for thirty-six straight hours!

Yayoi Kusama turned ninety-one in 2020, but she is still full of ideas. Many of her recent works include messages about world love and peace.

Yayoi wrote in her autobiography, "My plan has been to live exactly as I wanted to. I have been able to do just that, and I am glad I chose the road I did."

Yayoi worked hard and never gave up on her dreams to become a successful artist. Now that you've met Yayoi Kusama, wouldn't you like to do the same?

BUT WAIT...

THERE'S MORE!

Turn the page to learn about other popular female artists, fun art facts, the geography of Japan, and how to create your own work of art!

Other Popular Female Artists

Georgia O'Keeffe

Georgia O'Keeffe was born on a farm near Sun Prairie, Wisconsin, in 1887. Like Yayoi, she started drawing and painting at a young age. Georgia went on to study art in Chicago and New York City, where she soon captured the attention of many other artists. Georgia was very interested in nature, and after several years of painting in New York, she decided to travel around the United States, and eventually moved to New Mexico. Georgia loved painting the beautiful hills, flowers, and landscapes of the desert. In 1977, she received the Presidential Medal of Freedom, and today she is called "the mother of American modernism."

Frida Kahlo

Frida Kahlo was born in Coyoacán, Mexico City, Mexico, in 1907. When Frida was eighteen, she was in a bus accident that left her with serious injuries. During her recovery time at home, she began to paint. Because she had to stay in bed to get well, her parents mounted a mirror to the top of her bed, and she painted self-portraits. In 1929, Frida married the famous Mexican muralist Diego Rivera, whom she had met a few years earlier. The two of them traveled to many places, such as Paris and New York City, where Frida continued to paint. Frida still had health problems throughout her life, but that never stopped her from painting.

Art by the Numbers

There are many fine art degrees you can earn in college if you want to be an artist. Here are some of them.

- Sculpture
- Drawing and Painting
- Studio Arts
- Architecture
- Printmaking
- Digital Media
- Art History
- Photography
- Film/TV Production
- Animation
- Fashion Design
- Interior Design
- Graphic Design
- Art Design
- Creative Writing

Historians say that a type of pencil was used in ancient Greece. Some people believe the first wooden pencil was invented in 1560, but no one knows for sure.

Archaeologists (say: ar-KEY-ah-luh-jists), people who study past human life and artifacts, believe the first representation of art was made more than forty thousand years ago.

There are more than fifteen definitions of "art" in the *Oxford English Dictionary*!

Vincent van Gogh sold only one piece of art in his lifetime. Now he is one of the most famous painters in the world.

The second-largest sculpture in the world is Mount Rushmore, which took fourteen years to complete.

Japan

Matsumoto rests at the foot of the Japanese Alps. It is known for the historic Matsumoto Castle that was built in the 1500s.

Kyoto was once the capital of Japan. Today it embraces the heart of traditional Japanese culture and is popular for its stunning gardens, traditional temples and shrines, and specialty cuisine.

Tokyo is the current capital of Japan. It is one of the most populated cities in the world, and boasts a unique blend of traditional and contemporary cultures. In 2017, the Yayoi Kusama Museum opened in Tokyo.

The four largest cities in Japan are Tokyo, Yokohama, Osaka, and Nagoya.

MATSUMOTO
KYOTO ★ TOKYO
★
OSAKA ★ NAGOYA ★
★ YOKOHAMA